Angel Crafts

Publications International, Ltd.

CONTRIBUTING DESIGNERS:

Laura Holtorf Collins is a designer and writer specializing in needlecrafts. Besides her freelance business, she has previously served as department head of the crafts division at *Better Homes & Gardens* Special Interest Publications. Her designs appear on pages 19, 42, and 60.

Ricë Freeman-Zachery is a writer, teacher, and rubber-stamp artist who teaches college English and writes regularly for *RUBBERSTAMPMADNESS* Magazine. Her design appears on page 40.

Jane Johnston specializes in jewelry making and sells her craft designs to retail stores throughout southwestern Pennsylvania. She is a member of the Craftsman's Guild of Pittsburgh. Her designs appear on pages 49 and 54.

Tracia Ledford has designed for the craft and gift industry for more than 12 years. While her favorite medium is decorative painting, she also works with florals and fabric. She is a member of the Society of Craft Designers. Her designs appear on pages 24, 37, 47, 57, and 62.

Maria Nerius designs for retail outlets and manufacturers. Her woodcraft, doll, and jewelry designs have appeared in many craft publications, and have won honors in shows across the country. Ms. Nerius is a Certified Professional Demonstrator. Her designs appear on pages 12, 14, 17, 28, and 51.

Dee Dee Triplett is an award-winning designer with twenty years of experience designing, publishing, and teaching arts and crafts. Her special interests are fiber arts and dollmaking. She is a member of the Society of Craft Designers, and is a Certified Craft Designer. Her designs appear on pages 21, 31, 34, and 45.

Photography: Sacco Productions Limited/Chicago

Photographer: Peter Dean Ross

Photo Stylist: Melissa Frisco

Production: Paula M. Walters

Models: Karen Blaschek/Royal Model Management
Susan and Veronica Nigh/Stewart Talent Management

Technical Advisor: Christine DeJulio

Photo sites: Park St. Claire/Hoffman Homes, Schaumburg, IL
Wadsworth Development/Baxter Homes, Waukegan, IL

The mention of any product is merely a record of the procedure used and does not constitute an endorsement by the respective proprietors of Publications International, Ltd., nor does it constitute an endorsement by any of these companies that their products should be used in the manner recommended by this publication.

Products used by:
Laura Holtorf Collins: DMC embroidery floss; Kreinik blending filament, cable, braid, and ribbon; Westrim Crafts beads.
Ricë Freeman-Zachery: Leavenworth Jackson stamp; Marks of Distinction stamp.
Jane Johnston: Fimo polymer clay varnish.
Tracia Ledford: Aleene's OK to Wash It fabric glue; Delta Technical Coatings, Inc. acrylic paint and textile medium; Kunin Felt Company, Inc. felt; Plaid Enterprises Stiffy fabric stiffener; Lion Ribbon Company ribbons; Mark Enterprises glitter; St. Louis Trimming, Inc. trims; Therm O Web Heat n' Bond fabric adhesive and light fabric adhesive; Tulip Productions dimensional fabric paint; Wimpole Street Creations doll and hair.
Maria Nerius: Adhesive Technologies, Inc. Magic Melt glue and glue gun; Delta Technical Coatings, Inc. Creamcoat paint and varnish, and stencil paints; Fiskar Manufacturing Corp. scissors and tools; Loew Cornell paint and stencil brushes and stylus; Walnut Hollow Wood Crafts shelf and doll kits; Wimpole Street Creations doll hair products; JHB International miniatures and charms; Mitchell Marketing, Inc. wire angel wings; Sakura IDendti-pen brand permanent ink marking pens.
Dee Dee Triplett: Berol Prismacolor pencils; Delta Technical Coatings, Inc. fabric dyes; Friendly Plastic; Pellon fleece and Wonder-Under; UltraSuede.

Contents

Introduction
4

Introduction

Let more angels into your life with Angel Crafts! With different crafts to choose from, you'll find many projects to make for your home or to give as gifts. You'll find stitching, sewing, and painting crafts, and much more!

We hope you enjoy creating these projects. They are for all skill levels and interests. You'll find that many of the projects use basic items you already have around your home. Once you begin, you'll see that creating your own gifts and holiday decorations is satisfying and relaxing!

What You'll Find

Jewelry Making

Although the jewelry in this book looks sophisticated, most are made by gluing. Jewelry findings is a term for a variety of ready-made metal components used as attachments and fastenings to assemble a piece of jewelry. They are usually made of inexpensive metal. Findings include pin backs, earring findings, barrel clasps, jump rings, and beading wire. All of these items are easily found in your local craft or hobby store.

Cross-Stitch

Cross-stitch is traditionally worked on an "even-weave" cloth that has vertical and horizontal threads of equal thickness and spacing. Six-strand embroidery floss is used for most stitching; there are also many beautiful threads that can be used to enhance the appearance of the stitching. Finishing and framing a counted cross-stitch piece will complete your work. There are many options in framing—just visit your local craft shop or framing gallery.

Basic Supplies

Fabric: The most common even-weave fabric is 14-count Aida cloth. The weave of this fabric creates distinct squares that make stitching very easy for the beginner.

Needles, hoops, and scissors: A blunt-end or tapestry needle is used for counted cross-stitch. A #24 needle is the recommended size for stitching on 14-count Aida cloth. You may use an embroidery hoop while stitching—just be sure to remove it when not working on your project. A small pair of sharp scissors is a definite help when working with embroidery floss.

Floss: Six-strand cotton embroidery floss is most commonly used, and it's usually cut into 18-inch lengths for stitching. Use two of the six strands for stitching on 14-count Aida cloth. Also use two strands for backstitching.

Preparing to Stitch

The charts in this book will tell you what size the overall stitched area will be when completed. It will also tell you what size piece of cloth to use.

To locate the center of the design, lightly fold your fabric in half and in half again. Find the center of the chart by following the arrows on the sides.

Reading the chart is easy, since each square on the chart equals one stitch on the fabric. The colors correspond to the floss numbers listed in the color key. Select a color and stitch all of that color within an area. Begin by holding the thread ends behind the fabric until secured or covered over with two or three stitches. You may skip a few stitches on the back of the material, but do not run the thread from one area to another behind a section that will not be stitched in the finished piece—it will show through the fabric. If your thread begins to twist, drop the needle and allow the thread to untwist. It is important to the final appearance of the project to keep an even tension when pulling stitches through so that all stitches will have a uniform look. To end a thread, weave or run the thread under several stitches on the back side. Cut the ends close to the fabric.

Each counted cross-stitch is represented by a colored square on the project's chart. For horizontal rows, work the stitches in two steps, i.e., all of the left to right stitches and then all of the right to left stitches (see Figure A). For vertical rows, work each complete stitch as shown in Figure B. Three-quarter stitches are often used when the design requires two colors in one square or to allow more detail in the pattern (See Figure C). The backstitch is often used to outline or create letters, and is shown by bold lines on the patterns. Backstitch is usually worked after the pattern is completed (See Figure D).

Figure A
Cross-Stitch

Figure B
Vertical Cross-Stitch

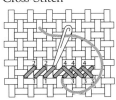

Figure C
Three-Quarter Stitch

Figure D
Backstitch

Figure E
French Knot

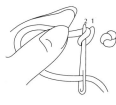

Bring thread up at 1. Wrap thread around needle and insert needle at 2, holding end of thread with fingers of hand not used for stitching. Tighten knot, then pull needle through fabric, holding thread until it must be released.

Plastic Canvas

Plastic canvas allows for three-dimensional stitchery projects to be constructed. Stitching on plastic canvas is easy to do, easy on the eyes, and easy on the pocketbook, too.

Basic Supplies

Plastic canvas: Canvas is most widely available by the sheet. Stitch all the pieces of a project on the same brand of plastic canvas to ensure that the meshes will match when you join them together.

Plastic canvas comes in several counts or mesh sizes (number of stitches to the inch) and numerous sizes of sheets. Specialty sizes and shapes such as circles are also available. Most canvas is clear, although up to 24 colors are available. Colored canvas is used when parts of the project remain unstitched. Seven-count canvas comes in four weights—standard; a thinner flexible weight; a stiffer, rigid weight; and a softer weight made especially for bending and curved projects. Designs can be stitched on any mesh count—the resulting size of the project is the only thing that will be affected. The smaller the count number, the larger the project will be, since the count number refers to the number of stitches per inch. Therefore, seven-count has seven stitches per inch, while 14-count has 14. A 14-count project will be half the size of a 7-count project if two identical projects were stitched on 7-count and 14-count canvas.

Needles: Needle size is determined by the count size of the plastic canvas you are using. Patterns generally call for a #18 needle for stitching on 7-count plastic canvas, a #16 or #18 for 10-count canvas, and a #22 or #24 for stitching on 14-count plastic canvas.

Yarns: A wide variety of yarns may be used. The most common is worsted weight (or 4-ply). Acrylic yarns are less expensive and washable; wool may also be used. Several companies produce specialty yarns for plastic canvas work. These cover the canvas well and will not "pill" as some acrylics do. Sport weight yarn (or 3-ply) and embroidery floss are often used on 10-count canvas. Use 12 strands or double the floss thickness for 10-count canvas and 6 strands for stitching on 14-count canvas. On 14-count plastic canvas, many of the specialty metallic threads made for cross-stitch can be used to highlight and enhance your project.

Cutting Out Your Project

Many plastic canvas projects are dimensional—a shape has to cut out and stitched.

Preparing to Stitch

Cut your yarn to a 36-inch length. Begin by holding the yarn end behind the fabric until secured or covered over with two or three stitches. To end a length, weave or run the yarn under several stitches on the back side. Cut the end close to the canvas. The continental stitch is the most commonly used stitch to cover plastic canvas. Decorative stitches will add interest and texture to your project. As in cross-stitch, if your yarn begins to twist, drop the needle and allow the yarn to untwist. Do not carry one color yarn across too many rows of another color on the back—the carried color may show through to the front. Do not stitch the outer edge of the canvas until the other stitching is complete. If the project is a single piece of canvas, overcast the outer edge with the color specified. If there are two or more pieces, follow the pattern instructions for assembly.

Cleaning

If projects are stitched with acrylic yarn, they may be washed by hand using warm or cool water and a mild detergent. Place on a terry cloth towel to air dry. Do not place in a dryer or dry clean.

The following stitches are used in plastic canvas:

Continental Stitch

For the continental stitch, your needle comes up at 1 and all odd-numbered holes, and goes down at 2 and all even-numbered holes.

Backstitch

Work the plastic canvas backstitch just as you do a cross-stitch backstitch.

Cross-Stitch

Work the plastic canvas cross-stitch just as you do a regular cross-stitch.

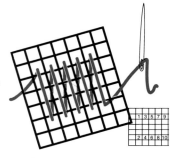

Gobelin Stitch

For the gobelin stitch, your needle comes up at 1 and all odd-numbered holes, and goes down at 2 and all even-numbered holes.

French Knot

For the French knot, bring your needle up at a hole and wrap yarn clockwise around needle. Holding the yarn, insert needle in the hole to the right and slowly pull yarn.

Overcast Stitch

For the overcast stitch, the needle goes down at the numbered holes, and the yarn wraps over the edge of the canvas. Make sure to cover the canvas completely.

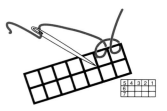

Wearables

You'll find fabric painting to be fast, easy, and fun. With the latest development in fabric paints, using basic dimensional paints is almost as easy as writing with a ballpoint pen. Some of the painting projects will require a brush—we'll tell you what type of brush you'll need in the project's materials list.

Protecting Your Project

You can use waxed paper ironed to the inside of the shirt to prevent paint from bleeding. You can also use a shirt board or you can make your own by cutting corrugated cardboard. Cover it with waxed paper and insert it into the item you'll be working on. Make sure the waxed side is under the surface you want to paint.

Paints

Each of the projects will specify the type of paints required. Only dimensional and embellished paints, which are especially formulated to use on fabric, are used. For specific instructions for each paint, follow the instructions on the packaging or bottle.

Basic Guidelines for Wearables

✳ Prewash fabric and sweatshirt without using any fabric softeners. Softeners prevent the paint from bonding completely with the fibers. Press out any wrinkles.

✳ If you're right-handed, work on your project from the upper left-hand corner to the lower right-hand corner. Paint all colors as you go. This will prevent you from accidentally smearing the paint with your elbow or hand.

✳ When using dimensional paints, pick up the tube of paint with the cap on and shake the paint down into the tip to remove any air bubbles each time you use a color. Place a paint bottle down on its side between uses.

✳ Hold your dimensional paint bottle like a ballpoint pen. Squeeze gently to push out paint. Work quickly and smoothly. Moving too slowly often results in a "bumpy" appearance.

✳ When using dimensional glitter paint, be sure to draw a line of paint that is thick enough to carry the glitter.

✳ Allow paints to dry at least 6 to 8 hours before touching. Allow 36 to 48 hours for paint to be completely cured before wearing.

Caring for Your Wearable

Hand or machine wash in lukewarm water—NOT COLD!!—in delicate/knit cycle. Cold water will crack the paint. Tumble dry on low for a few minute to remove wrinkles, then remove and lay flat to dry. Do not wash in Woolite or other delicate care products.

Sewing

The excitement of making your own holiday crafts sometimes gets in the way of your preparation. Before plunging into your chosen project, check to make sure you have all the materials needed. Being prepared will make your sewing easier and more fun. Most of the items you need will probably be on hand already.

Scissors: Two styles are needed, one about eight to ten inches long with a bent handle for cutting fabric. This style of scissors allows you to cut through the fabric while the fabric lays flat. These shears should be sharp and used only for fabric. The second style of scissors is smaller, about six inches, with sharp points. You will need this style for smaller projects and close areas.

Straight pins: Nonrusting dressmaker pins are best to use. They will not leave rust marks on your fabric if they come in contact with dampness or glue. And dressmaker pins have very sharp points for easy insertion.

Tape measure: Should be plastic coated so that it will not stretch and could be wiped off if it comes in contact with paint or glue.

Ironing board and steam iron: Be sure your ironing board is well padded and has a clean covering. Sometimes you do more sewing with the iron than you do with the sewing machine. Keeping your fabrics, seams, and hems pressed cuts down on stitches and valuable time. A steam or dry iron is best. It is important to press your fabric to achieve a professional look. The iron is also used to adhere the fusible interfacing. Keep the bottom of your iron clean and free of any substance that could mark your fabric. The steam iron may be used directly on most fabrics with no shine. Test a small piece of the fabric first. If it causes a shine on the right side, try the reverse side.

Thread: Have mercerized sewing thread in the colors needed for each project. Proper shade and strength (about a 50 weight) of thread avoids having the stitching show more than is necessary.

Fusible interfacing (or webbing): The webbing is placed paper side up on wrong side of material. Place iron on paper side of adhesive and press for one to three seconds. Allow fabric to cool. Design can then be drawn or traced onto the paper side and cut out. Remove the paper and place the material right side up in desired position on project and iron for three to five seconds.

Sewing machine: Neat, even stitches are achieved in a very few minutes with a sewing machine, which helps you complete your project with ease. If desired, you may machine stitch a zigzag stitch around the attached fusible adhesive pieces to secure the edges.

Work surface: Your sewing surface should be a comfortable height for sitting and roomy enough to lay out your projects. Keep it clean and free of other crafting materials that could accidently spill.

A Word About Glue

Glue can be a sticky subject when you don't use the right one for the job. There are many different glues on the craft market today, each formulated for a different crafting purpose. The following are ones you should be familiar with:

White glue: This may be used as an all-purpose glue—it dries clear and flexible. It is often referred to as craft glue or tacky glue. Tacky on contact, it allows you to put two items together without a lot of set-up time required. Use for most projects, especially ones involving wood, plastics, some fabrics, and cardboard.

Thin-bodied glues: Use these glues when your project requires a smooth, thin layer of glue. Thin-bodied glues work well on some fabrics and papers.

Fabric glue: This type of glue is made to bond with fabric fibers and withstand repeated washing. Use this kind of glue for attaching rhinestones and/or other charms to fabric projects. Some glues require heat-setting. Check the bottle for complete instructions.

Hot melt glue: Formed into cylindrical sticks, this glue is inserted into a hot temperature glue gun and heated to liquid state. Depending on the type of glue gun used, the glue is forced out through the gun's nozzle by either pushing on the end of the glue stick or squeezing a trigger. Use clear glue sticks for projects using wood, fabrics, most plastics, ceramics, and cardboard. When using any glue gun, be careful of the nozzle and the freshly applied glue—it is very hot! Apply glue to the piece being attached. Work with small areas at a time so that the glue doesn't set before being pressed into place.

Low melt glue: This is similar to hot melt glues in that it is formed into sticks and requires a glue gun to be used. Low melt glues are used for projects that would be damaged by heat. Examples include foam, balloons, and metallic ribbons. Low melt glue sticks are oval-shaped and can only be used in a low temperature glue gun.

The Band Saw

The band saw is a very handy, easy-to-use tool for the home workshop. It may be easily operated by a man, woman, or an older child with supervision. A band saw may sit on your workbench or it may also have its own legs or stand. Also, it does not take up much space.

Respect your band saw—Safety First! Before you begin to saw, read your instruction manual. Always keep in mind these simple safety hints:

* Keep your work area clean and uncluttered.
* Don't use band saw in damp or wet locations.
* Keep your work area well-lit.
* Do not force the band saw to saw through items that it is not designed for.
* Wear proper clothing—nothing loose or baggy.
* Wear safety goggles.
* Never leave band saw running unattended.

One advantage of the band saw is its versatility. The fast cutting saw uses a flexible steel blade, in the form of a continuous loop, that runs over two rubber wheels. To use the saw, feed the wood into the blade. For straight, fast cutting, use a wide coarse-toothed blade, for curve cutting, use a narrower blade. Don't try to turn corners that are too tight for the blade width; if you do the blade will burn and the wood may become wedged onto the saw blade. The $^3/_{26}$-inch blade will cut a one-inch circle, the $^1/_2$-inch blade will cut a $2^1/_2$-inch circle, and the $^3/_4$-inch blade will cut a $3^1/_2$-inch circle.

When operating the saw, set the upper blade guide about $^1/_4$ to $^1/_2$ inch above the work. Band saw blades are reasonably priced and stay sharp a long time. It is practical to throw away the old ones rather than to sharpen them. Never use a dull blade!

Most band saws are equipped with a tilting table for beveling and for cutting objects at an angle. Sometimes it is necessary to turn the work upside down to make certain parts of a cut. After practicing with your band saw, you will become more comfortable with it.

Decorative Wood Painting
Paints
There are a wide variety of paint brands to choose from. Acrylic paints are available at your local arts and crafts stores in a wide variety of brands. Mix and match your favorite colors to paint the projects in this book. These projects will work with any acrylic paint brands.

Acrylic paint dries in minutes and allows projects to be completed in no time at all. Clean hands and brushes with soap and water.

Some projects may require a medium that is not acrylic or water based. These require mineral spirits to clean up. Always check the manufacturer's label before working with a product so you can have the proper supplies available.

Finishes
Choose from a wide variety of types and brands of varnishes to protect your finished project. Varnish is available in both spray and brush on.

Brush on water-based varnishes dry in minutes and clean up with soap and water. Use over any acrylic paints. Don't use over paints or mediums requiring mineral spirits clean up.

Spray varnishes can be used over any type of paint or medium. For projects with a pure white surface, choose a nonyellowing varnish. The slight yellowing of some varnishes can actually enhance certain projects for a richer look. Varnishes are available in matte, satin, or gloss finishes. Choose the shine you prefer.

Brushes and Paint Supplies
Foam (sponge) brushes work great to seal, basecoat, and varnish wood. Clean foam brushes with soap and water when using acrylic paints and mediums. For paints or mediums that require mineral spirits to clean up, you will have to throw the disposable brush away.

Synthetic brushes work well with acrylic paints for details and designs. You will use a liner brush for thin lines and details. A script brush is needed for extra long lines. Round brushes fill in round areas, stroke work, and broad lines. An angle brush is used to fill in large areas, float, or side-load color. A large flat brush is used to apply basecoat and varnish. Small flat brushes are for stroke work and basecoating small areas.

Wood Preparation
Properly preparing your wood piece can make all the difference in the outcome. Having a smooth surface to work on will allow you to complete the project quickly and easily. Once the wood is prepared, you are ready to proceed with a basecoat, stain, or finish, according to the project instructions. Some finishes, such as crackling, will recommend not sealing the wood. Always read instructions completely before starting.

Supplies you will need to prepare the wood: sand paper (#200) for removing roughness; tack cloth, which is a sticky resin-treated cheese cloth, to remove dust after sanding; a wood sealer to seal wood and prevent warping; and a foam or 1-inch flat brush to apply sealer.

Floating Color

This technique is also called side loading. It is used to shade or highlight the edge of an object. Floated color is a gradual blend of color to water.

1. Moisten an angle or flat brush with water. Blot excess water from brush, setting bristles on paper towel until shine of water disappears.

2. Dip the long corner of angle brush into paint. Load paint sparingly. Carefully stroke brush on palette until color blends halfway across the brush. If the paint blends all the way to short side, clean and load again. For thicker paint, dilute first with 50 percent water.

3. Hold the brush at a 45 degree angle, and using a light touch, apply color to designated area.

Dots

Perfect round dots can be made with any round implement. The size of the implement determines the size of the dot. You can use the wooden end of a brush, a stylus tip, a pencil tip, or the eraser end of pencil (with an unused eraser).

1. Use undiluted paint for thick dots or dilute paint with 50 percent water for smooth dots. Dip the tip into paint and then onto the surface. For uniform dots, you must redip in paint for each dot. For graduated dots, continue dotting with same paint load. Clean tip on paper towel after each group and reload.

2. To create hearts, place two dots of the same size next to each other. Then drag paint from each dot down to meet in bottom of heart. To create teddy bears from dots, follow sequence of dots in picture.

Stenciling

This is a method of painting using plastic with shapes cut in it. Simply apply paint inside the shapes with a stencil brush for perfect designs. A sponge or old brush with bristles cut short will also work.

1. Use a precut stencil pattern or make your own. Draw a design on plastic and cut out with a craft knife. Tape on surface or spray back of stencil with stencil adhesive.

2. Don't thin the paint. Dip tip of a stencil brush in paint. Blot paint off on paper towel. Too much paint or too watery paint can bleed under stencil. Practice on paper first.

3. Hold brush in an upright position, pounce repeatedly inside cut out area. Make color heavy on the edges and sparse in the center for a shaded look.

Knob-and-Pole Printing

This is one of the simplest ways to create decorative printing for the beginner. Letters are made up of thin lines and dots. Practice on paper.

1. Print letters lightly on surface with pencil. Line the letters with desired paint color. Use undiluted paint for thick lines or thin with 50 percent water for thin lines.

2. Add a dot on each bend and ends of letters. For O, place dot on top, a bit to the left of center.

Making A Multiloop Bow

There are many ways to make bows, and the more you make, the easier it becomes. Follow the instructions, and before long you will be a pro.

1. Crimp the ribbon between thumb and forefinger at the desired streamer length, with the streamer hanging down. Make an equal number of loops on each side of your thumb by

crimping each individually while you guide the ribbon into a loop in a circular direction. Crimp each new loop next to the previous one, rather than on top. Secure the loops in the center with wire twisted tightly on the back, leaving the second streamer pointing up.

2. While holding the bow in the same position, roll three inches of that streamer toward you over your thumb, making a small center loop as a knot. If the ribbon has a right and wrong

side, twist the loop right side out and catch the loop under your thumb. The streamer will again be pointing up. Bring one end of wire from the back over that streamer beside the knot and to the back again. Twist the wires again. Bring the streamers together beneath the bow and V- or angle-cut the ends at different lengths.

To make your bows more professional, here are two ways to cut ribbon ends:
To V-cut ribbon, gently fold the ribbon ends in half lengthwise. Cut from the outside edge up toward the fold.
To angle-cut ribbon, cut the ends at an angle in either direction.

Whimsical
Wreath of Gold

Golden, precious treasures don't always cost lots of money—a little time, a few supplies, and some love is all you need to create this heartwarming wreath!

* 10-inch wreath
* 2½ yards mini gold star garland
* Low-temp glue and glue gun
* 44 inches wine wire-edged ribbon, 2 inches wide
* Scissors
* 24-gauge gold wire
* Wire cutters
* 1 sun button
* 1 moon button
* 4 star charms
* Pencil or pen
* 3 wood peg dolls
* Acrylic paint: flesh, medium flesh, dark flesh
* Gold glitter paint
* Paintbrush
* 15 inches flat white lace, ½ inch wide
* Tacky glue
* Gold slivers or glitter
* Chenille stem

1. Attach an end of garland to back of wreath with low-temp glue. Wrap garland around wreath, securing end with glue. Cut 32 inches from wine ribbon. Make a simple 5-inch bow. Trim tails with a vertical cut. Glue bow to top of wreath. Tack tails to wreath with glue.

2. Cut 24-gauge wire into three 12-inch pieces. Thread moon and sun buttons (one on each end) onto wire. Secure buttons to wire with several twists. On other pieces of wire, repeat this process for star charms. Curl wire by wrapping the wire around a pencil or pen. Slip pencil from wire. Gently pull ends of wires to relax curls. Fold wire at center. Glue folded end of wire and insert into the top inside of wreath beneath bow.

3. Paint heads of peg dolls with flesh tones. Apply second coat if needed. Paint bodies of peg dolls with glitter paint. Several coats are needed for full coverage. Let dry.

4. Cut flat lace into three 4-inch pieces. If lace has a motif (flower or heart), cut 3 patterns out of remaining lace. Glue lace pieces to bottom of peg doll bodies with tacky glue. Glue motif to doll at front neckline.

5. Apply a circle of tacky glue to top of doll head and fill in circle. Dip doll head into gold slivers to create hair. Shake off excess. Let dry.

6. Cut remaining wine ribbon into three 4-inch pieces. Cut chenille stem into 3 pieces. Fold one 4-inch ribbon in half, then unfold. Fold each raw end of ribbon into center fold. Gather at center and tie off with chenille stem. Trim excess chenille stem. Puff up wings. Glue wings to back of peg doll with glue gun. Repeat for other wings.

7. Attach angels to inside bottom of wreath with low-temp glue. Adjust sun, moon, and stars to fall around angels.

An Angel for All Seasons

Keep angels in your house all year round! You can dress up this angel for Easter, Christmas, fall, spring, or any other occasion. Come up with your own basket ideas for a one-of-a-kind touch!

* Small Walnut Hollow Darling Doll
* Water-based acrylic wood sealer
* Acrylic paint: flesh, cardinal red, blue jay, black
* Flat paintbrush
* Stylus
* Paper palette
* Tacky glue
* 11 inches white flat lace, ½ inch wide
* 11 × 3½-inch piece white fabric
* Sewing machine and scissors
* Iron
* 3-inch white doily
* 8 feet white ribbon, 1/16 inch wide
* Doll hair
* Miniature gold heart charm
* 6-inch wire angel wings
* Staple gun
* 2 inches white tulle bow
* 5 mini chipwood baskets
* Christmas: 1-inch pine tree, four 1-inch candy canes, 6-inch string miniature lights
* Fall: five 1½-inch leaves, two ¾-inch pumpkins
* Spring: dried flowers, 1-inch butterfly
* Easter: four ¾-inch wood eggs, purple excelsior
* Apple: five ½-inch apples
* 5 painted ¾-inch hearts: red, orange, mauve, pink, green

1. Paint wood sealer on all wooden pieces. Basecoat doll body and head with flesh paint. Float red cheeks on doll face. Dot blue eyes with stylus (see page 10). Allow to dry. Paint shoes black. Glue shoes to doll legs.

2. Sew flat lace to bottom raw edge of fabric. Iron dress flat if needed. Fold dress in half with right sides together and sew back seam with 1/8-inch seam allowance. Before turning dress, cut 2-inch arm slit at center top of dress. Turn dress.

3. Working back to front (with seam at back), fold arm slit sides in ¼ inch and neckline down ¼ inch. Finger press folds. Sew a running stitch across top of neckline. Slip dress on body. Pull gathers firmly, leaving a ½-inch circle for doll head to be glued at top of body. Knot off.

4. Glue doily to top of doll body, letting it fall equally in front and back. Glue doll head to center of doily. Allow glue to set.

5. Cut white ribbon into five 12-inch, one 7-inch, one 5-inch, and eight 4-inch pieces. Set 12-inch pieces aside for baskets. Tie the 5-inch ribbon tightly around doll hair 1 inch from one raw end (bangs). Randomly tie 4-inch pieces of white ribbons to doll hair making simple hair bows. Trim ribbon bows. Thread 7-inch ribbon through heart charm, securing heart to center of ribbon with knot. Place necklace around doll's neck and knot off. Apply a small puddle of glue to center top of doll head. Attach hair to doll head allowing for bangs. Allow glue to dry. Trim hair if needed.

6. Lift hair from back of angel and lay wings across back. Using staple gun, attach wings to angel back. Glue white tulle bow over staples. Bend halo down.

7. For baskets: Gather materials needed for each basket. Glue specified items into baskets.

8. Glue painted hearts to front of baskets: Red for Christmas, orange for fall, mauve for spring, pink for Easter, and green for apple.

9. Tie a ribbon to each basket. Attach basket to angel, threading an end of ribbon through back of arm hole and pulling through. Tie to secure.

Dizzy Izzy Clothespin Angels

Looking for child-safe ornaments that will also add humor and fun to your Christmas tree? Here are the angels for you—these amusing clip-ons will keep your children happy at tree-trimming time and they'll make the whole family laugh!

What You'll Need

* ❋ 1 × 4 × 2-inch wood for one
* ❋ Band or scroll saw
* ❋ Drill and ⅛ brad point drill bit
* ❋ Fine-grain sandpaper
* ❋ Acrylic paint: flesh, rouge, blue
* ❋ Flat paintbrush
* ❋ Stylus
* ❋ Iridescent shredded plastic
* ❋ Tacky glue
* ❋ Scissors
* ❋ Burgundy bow with gold bead
* ❋ 4½ inches flat lace, ½ inch wide
* ❋ 4½ × 1¼-inch piece Christmas fabric
* ❋ Sewing machine
* ❋ Iron
* ❋ Needle and thread
* ❋ 3-inch wire wings
* ❋ Mini clip clothespin
* ❋ Small satin bow

1. Cut out doll body with saw. Drill hair holes as indicated on pattern. Sand body smooth.

2. Basecoat doll body with flesh paint. Paint cheeks rouge. Using stylus, dot eyes with blue or your choice of eye color. Allow to dry.

3. Take some strands of plastic and twist bottoms of the strands together, making a point. Apply glue into hair hole and insert hair with tweezers or fingers. Allow glue to set. Repeat for all holes. Trim hair. Glue burgundy bow to head.

4. Sew lace to a raw edge of fabric. Iron dress flat. Fold dress in half (right sides together) and sew a back seam. Turn dress right side out. Fold

neckline down ¼ inch. Starting at seam, sew a running stitch across top of dress. Place dress on doll body. Pull gathers firmly to doll and knot off with seam at back of doll.

5. Apply a thin line of glue along seam of dress. Allow glue to air-dry a few minutes to become more tacky. Attach wire wings to doll and hold wings in place until glue sets.

6. Apply a thin line of glue to bottom of angel body. Attach mini clothespin to bottom. Allow glue to set. Glue satin bow to front of clothespin. Allow 24 hours to dry before using ornament.

Cross-Stitched Winged Angel

This elegant angel will add sparkle and beauty to any setting. She may test your cross-stitch skills while you work on her, but she is well worth the effort!

What You'll Need

* ✳ 9 × 12-inch sheet white perforated paper, #14
* ✳ 1 skein each embroidery floss: pale peach, medium pink, light pink, blue, dark brown, burgundy, light yellow, medium yellow, light brown, rose-coral, teal, plum
* ✳ Tapestry needle
* ✳ 1 reel each blending filament: lavender, yellow
* ✳ 1 reel gold cable, 10m

For face and neck, use 1 strand pale peach. Use 1 strand medium pink for cheeks. Use 1 strand light pink for lower neck. Use 1 strand blue for eyes. Use 1 strand dark brown with 1 strand lavender filament to outline face, eyelids, and eyebrows. Use 1 strand dark brown to outline eyes and nose. Use 2 strands burgundy for mouth.

For hair, use 2 strands yellow filament with 1 strand light yellow floss for lighter areas. Use 2 strands of medium yellow floss for darker areas. Use 1 strand light brown to outline hair and neck.

To fill in upper wings, us 2 strands medium pink wit 1 strand lavender filament. To fill in middle area, use 1 strand medium pink with 2 strands lavender filament. To fill in lower area, use 4 strands lavender filament.

To outline wings, use 1 strand rose-coral floss with 2 strands lavender filament.

For collar, use 1 strand teal, 1 strand plum floss with 1 strand lavender filament, and 1 strand gold cable where indicated. Use 1 strand gold for halo.

▨	Rose coral
▨	Medium dark pink
▨	Gold cable
▨	Medium yellow

☐	Light yellow
▨	Teal
▨	Plum
☐	Light pink
☐	Lavender
☐	Medium pink
☐	Medium light pink
☐	Light brown
▨	Dark brown
▨	Burgundy
▨	Blue
☐	Pale peach

Sweet Scandinavian Angel

You don't need to be Scandinavian to appreciate the charm of this folksy angel. What kitchen wouldn't feel warmer with her in it?

What You'll Need

* ✳ 9 × 12-inch felt squares: 3 flesh, 1 blue, 1 white
* ✳ Press cloth
* ✳ 1 yard fusible webbing
* ✳ Pencil
* ✳ Scissors
* ✳ 27 inches cotton lace, ¼ inch wide
* ✳ Tacky glue
* ✳ DMC flower thread to match felt plus red
* ✳ 5 tiny heart appliqués
* ✳ ½ yard each red and white ribbon flowers (or 10 small red ribbon flowers; 14 small white ribbon flowers; 9 inches white ribbon, ⅛ inch wide)
* ✳ 1 small red bow
* ✳ 2 white embroidered leaves, 3 × 2¼ inches each
* ✳ 6 inches white ribbon, ⅛ inch wide

1. Using press cloth to cover felt, fuse 2 squares of flesh felt together, with webbing between. Trace outline of angel onto paper side of webbing. Fuse to last sheet of flesh felt. Cut angel out and remove paper. Fuse angel to doubled flesh piece. Cut angel out. Trace dress shape on paper of webbing. Fuse to blue felt and cut out. Trace, fuse, and cut out hat and apron from white felt. Remove all paper. Fuse dress to body. Trim ¼-inch lace to fit around apron edge. Place edge of lace

under edge of apron and fuse apron to dress. Glue lace at wrists. Fuse hat to head.

2. Using 1 strand of flower thread to match each felt color, work a buttonhole stitch around all edges except hat. Make blue French knots for eyes, and red for mouth.

3. Glue lace across bottom of skirt ¼ inch up from bottom edge. Glue hearts above lace. Glue a red flower to each foot. Glue 6 white flowers around hat. Glue red bow at waist.

4. Twist strands of 8 white and red ribbon flowers together to form garland (or sew or glue red and white ribbon flowers to ribbon). Tack garland ends to hands.

5. Sew or glue 2 embroidered leaves to back of shoulders for wings. Sew a white ribbon loop at back of head to hang.

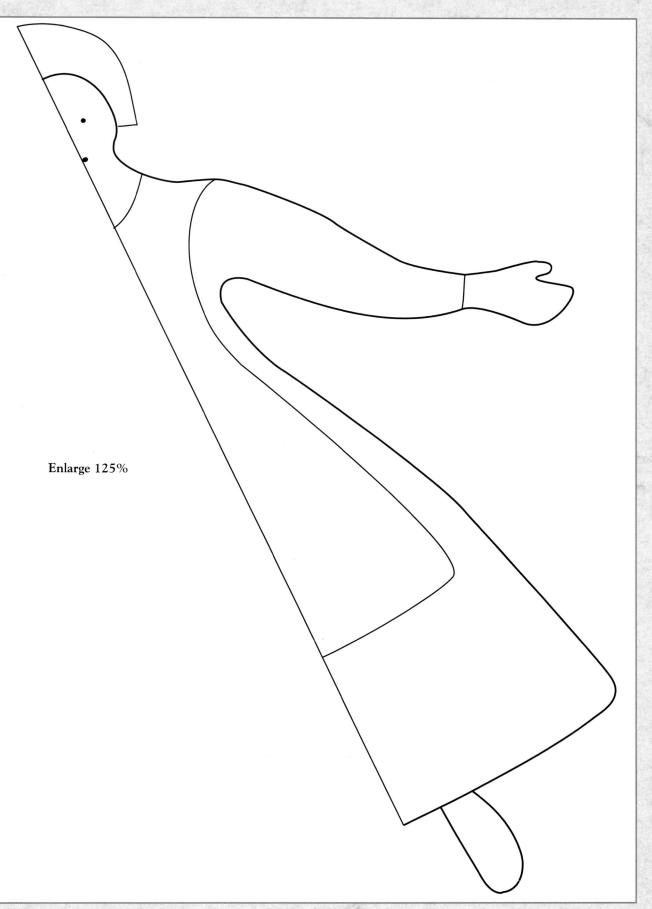

Enlarge 125%

Mamma and Her Angel

This adorable bib can be assembled and ready to put on your favorite angel in no time. And the t-shirt can be your reward to yourself, for all the wonderful things you do for those you love!

Angel Bib

What You'll Need

- ✳ Terrycloth bib (8 × 10 inches)
- ✳ 4-inch square muslin
- ✳ Tea bag and cup
- ✳ Iron-on fabric adhesive
- ✳ 4-inch square pastel calico fabric
- ✳ Iron
- ✳ Pencil
- ✳ Scissors
- ✳ Cardboard
- ✳ Masking tape
- ✳ Small stencil brush
- ✳ Acrylic red paint
- ✳ Paper towel
- ✳ Dimensional fabric paint: black slick, ivory pearl, gold glitter, gold pearl, pink pearl
- ✳ 10/0 liner brush

1. Dip muslin into cup of hot tea. Let dry; press. Iron adhesive to back of muslin and calico; press for 4 seconds. Enlarge pattern 167 percent on copier. Trace pattern on the back of the prepared materials. Cut shapes out and remove paper.

2. Press face, collar, and bow to bib, for 4 to 5 seconds, using medium setting. Tape bib to cardboard. Using small stencil brush, dip into red paint. Wipe brush clean with paper towel. Pounce cheeks on face using stencil brush.

3. Dot eyes with black slick fabric paint. Dip liner brush into black mixed with small amount of water and paint eyebrows, mouth, and nose. Dot cheek and eye highlights with ivory pearl using end of paintbrush. Draw halo with gold glitter paint.

4. Outline face with ivory pearl. Draw hair with gold pearl. Using pink pearl, outline collar and bow. Dot buttons under collar.

5. Write Lil Angel with pink pearl. Draw hearts with gold pearl. Let dry 8 hours.

T-shirt

What You'll Need

* White t-shirt
* ⅛ yard muslin
* 2 tea bags
* Iron
* ½ yard iron-on fabric adhesive
* ⅛ yard rose calico
* Scrap calico print (light background)
* Scissors
* Cardboard or t-shirt board
* Disappearing fabric pen
* Dimensional fabric paint: sparkles gold, gold glitter, liquid pearl, pink pearl, black
* Brushes: 10/0 liner, small stencil, #8 flat
* Acrylic paint: medium green, red
* Paper towel
* Gold crystal glitter with stars

1. Soak muslin for 2 minutes in pot of hot tea. Let dry; press. Iron adhesive to back of calicos and muslin, using medium setting. Press for 4 to 5 seconds. Enlarge pattern 167 percent on copier. Trace patterns on back of prepared materials (face, hands, legs, and bag on muslin; heart, dress, and shoes on rose calico; patches and sleeves on light calico). Cut out and remove paper. Iron pieces to t-shirt in order: head, dress, sleeves, hands, legs, shoes, bag, patches, and large heart. Place t-shirt over cardboard. Trace wing shapes onto t-shirt, using fabric pen.

2. Squirt 3 dime-size puddles of sparkles gold inside of each wing; spread smooth with flat brush. Paint grass around feet using liner brush with medium green. Dip stencil brush in red paint and wipe on paper towel until almost all of paint is removed. Pounce cheeks onto face.

3. Using gold glitter paint, outline halo, wings, bag, and large heart. Dot on buttons. Using liquid pearl paint, outline head, hands, and legs. Draw on socks. Using pink pearl paint, outline sleeves, dress, patches, and shoes. Draw hair bow, and dot flowers at feet.

4. Using black paint, draw hair, large heart handle, and dot eyes. Adding small amount of water to black paint and using liner brush, paint eyebrows, stitches on patches, bow on bag, and Angel Dust on bag using knob-and-pole printing (see page 11).

5. Squirt rainbow shape of sparkles gold paint around large heart and area coming out of bag. Spread with flat brush. Fill mouth of bag with sparkles gold paint. Carefully sprinkle star glitter on wet paint. Let shirt dry for 8 hours without moving it, then shake off excess glitter.

Large Heart

Angel Dust

Patches

Angel Folk Band

What could be better than a folk band to herald the
joy of Christmas? This charming and friendly bunch
of angels make beautiful music together!

What You'll Need

* 8 × ¾ × 15 inches wood
* Heavyweight paper and pencil
* Band or scroll saw
* Drill and ⅝-inch brad point drill
* Fine-grain sandpaper
* Acrylic paint: flesh, hydrangea pink, lilac, blue jay, cactus, dolphin grey, rouge, cardinal red, Monet blue, copen blue, dark brown
* #6 or #8 flat paintbrush
* Paper towel
* Paper palette
* Stylus
* Jute
* Scissors
* Tacky glue
* 1 yard each white, light blue, mint, mauve, pink ribbon; 1/16 inch wide
* ½ yard muslin
* ½ yard fleece or batting
* Needle and white thread
* Iron and spray starch
* 3 miniature instruments
* 4½-inch musical paper ribbon

1. Trace angel and wing patterns onto paper to make templates. Lightly trace angel patterns onto wood with pencil. Cut out angels with saw. Mark angels with pencil dots for hair holes. Drill hair holes ¼ inch deep. Sand angel bodies smooth.

2. Paint dresses onto angel bodies using colors indicated on patterns. Let dry. Apply second coat if needed. Paint head and hands flesh. Let dry. Apply second coat if needed.

3. Shade arms on angels with copen blue as shown on patterns. Dip a #6 or #8 flat brush into clean water. Tap brush on paper towel to remove excess water. Dip one corner of brush into copen blue and stroke back and forth on paper palette until color blends. Color on brush will be on the outside of arms. Shade arms on all angels.

4. Paint faces onto angels as indicated on patterns. Cheeks are floated (see page 10) or stylus dotted hearts. Use stylus to paint two dots side by side. At center of dots, pull paint down with point of stylus to form heart (see page 10). Dot eyes on faces. Note: Different expressions on faces can be achieved by placing eyes closer together and by painting eyes at different levels on face. The closer eyes are to each other and to cheeks, the more

whimsical the expression. Experiment on scrap paper.

5. Cut jute hair for angels. Angel A needs thirty 6-inch lengths. Apply glue into each hair hole. Insert 6 strands into each hole. Let dry. Braid hair to 1½ inches and secure end with ribbon. Angel B needs ten 2-inch lengths. Glue 2 strands into each hair hole. Let dry. Tie ribbon to base of each hair strand grouping. Angel C needs fifteen 3-inch lengths. Glue 3 strands into each hair hole. Let dry. Tie ribbon around end of each hair strand. Angel D needs five 4-inch lengths. Glue a strand into each hair hole. Let dry. Tie ribbon to end of each hair strand. Angel E needs five 2-inch lengths. Glue a strand into each hair hole. Let dry. Tie ribbon to end of each hair strand. Trim ribbons.

6. Cut out wings from muslin and batting. Sandwich batting between 2 muslin wings. Pin wings to hold batting in place. Starting at indentation at bottom of wing, quilt wings together with a running stitch. Knot off at starting knot. Complete all wings. Iron wings using spray starch to add body. Trim loose fibers and batting. Glue wings to angels.

7. Glue musical instrument to angels B, C, and E. Keep flat until glue dries. Glue musical paper ribbon to angel A and angel D and lay flat until glue dries.

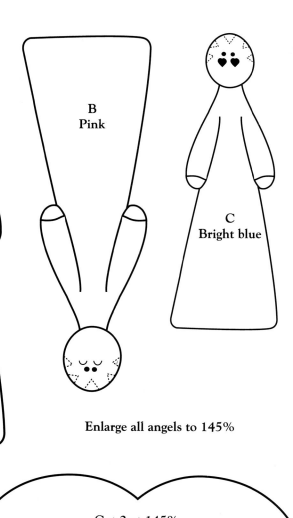

A
Blue-grey

B
Pink

C
Bright blue

Enlarge all angels to 145%

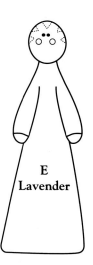

E
Lavender

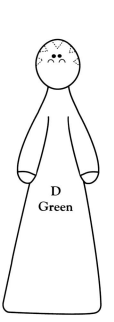

D
Green

Cut 2 at 145%
Cut 2 at 100%
Cut 2 at 90%

Cut 2 at 145%
Cut 2 at 100%

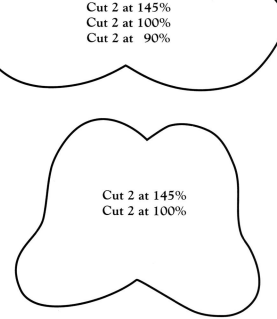

Chintz Guardian Angel

What better place for a guardian angel than over your bed? This beauty will remind you that you're being protected from above while decorating your room!

What You'll Need

* 1 yard peach colored chintz
* Tracing paper
* Pencil
* Scissors
* 6 lace motifs
* 1 yard fleece
* Fabric dyes: white, midnight, black
* Small artist's paintbrush
* Brown very fine-line permanent marker
* Color pencils: magenta, blush
* 1 lace medallion, about 3 × 3½ inches
* Sewing machine, matching thread
* 20 inches lace, 1¼ inches wide
* Tacky glue
* 26 ribbon flowers: mixture of ⅜ inch, ⅝ inch, ¾ inch, and 1⅛ inches in diameter

1. Enlarge pattern 200 percent. Place pieces of lace on wing pattern and arrange, altering shape of wings if necessary to fit motifs. Cut 2 angel shapes out of chintz, and 2 out of fleece.

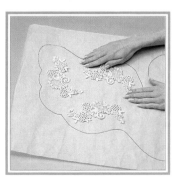

2. Trace face pattern onto a piece of chintz. Paint entire eye white; let dry. Paint iris with mixture of midnight and white; let dry. Paint pupils black, making a white highlight in each eye. Very lightly go over nose line with brown marker. Use brown marker for eyebrows, lashes, and to outline eyes. For lips, use magenta pencil. Softly color lips slightly darker in center and at top and bottom. Add blush to cheeks with blush pencil.

3. Pin angel front on top of 2 layers of fleece. Place and pin or baste lace motifs on wings and medallion in center. With thread that matches lace, sew on lace.

4. Place angel back right side down on top of face piece and pin. Sew around edge with ¼-inch seam allowance and leaving opening to turn. Clip seam allowances. Turn right side out. Blindstitch opening closed.

5. Slightly gather 15 inches of lace for hair and sew it around head on seam line. Make three thread loops on back for hanging.

6. Glue ribbon flowers and motifs cut from leftover hair lace on dotted line in center of angel.

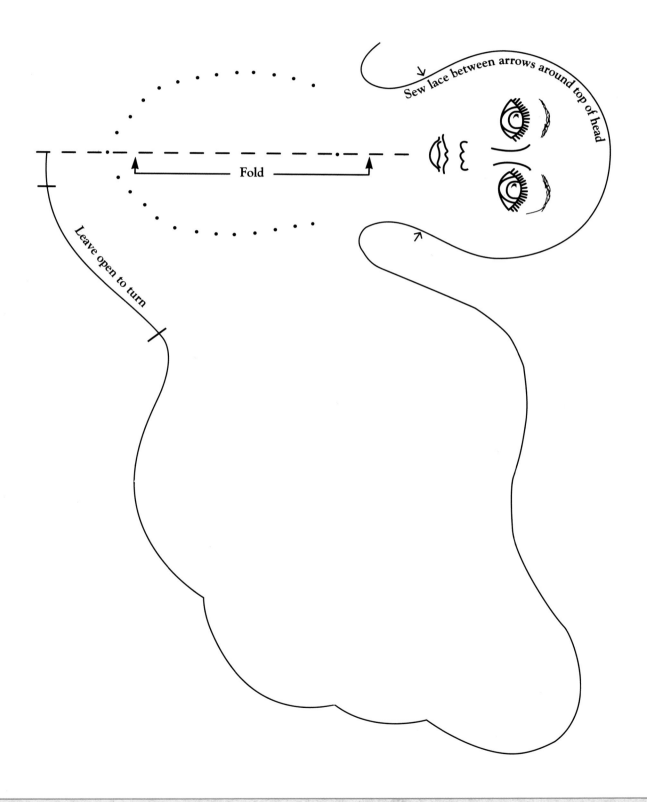

Sew lace between arrows around top of head

Fold

Leave open to turn

Classic Cutwork Angel

*What better way to herald the coming of the
Christmas season than with this lovely cutwork
angel. It's so beautiful you might want to hang it
year round!*

* 9 × 12-inch piece ivory ultrasuede
* 9 × 12-inch piece fusible webbing
* Press cloth
* Steam iron
* Scissors, sharp craft knife
* ⅝ yard blue cotton velveteen
* Sewing machine
* Needle, blue and white thread
* 12 × 15-inch piece fleece
* 18 inches gold metallic twisted cording, ³⁄₁₆ inch wide
* 3½-inch gold metallic tassel
* 22 ivory pearls, 3mm each
* 10½-inch length wooden dowel, ¼ inch diameter

1. Trace angel, halo, and arms onto paper side of webbing, marking areas that will be cut out with Xs. Fuse webbing to wrong side of ultrasuede, using a press cloth. Cut out angel. Cut out all areas marked with Xs.

2. Cut 18 × 23-inch rectangle of velveteen. Fold right sides together and sew a ½-inch seam allowance along 18-inch side. Refold so that seam is in center of tube. Mark and sew diagonal lines to shape bottom of banner. Trim corners and turn right side out; leaving top of banner open.

3. Cut one piece of fleece the same shape as the banner. Insert fleece into banner.

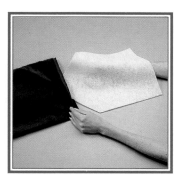

4. Center angel on banner. Cover with press cloth and using steam rather than pressure, fuse angel to banner. Fuse halo and leaf shapes from cutouts one at a time so they don't slip under press cloth. Fuse arms over area shown on pattern by dotted lines.

5. To finish banner, fold top 2½ inches of banner to back. Tucking under raw edges, hand sew to form a casing for dowel. Sew ends of cording in ends of casing for hanger. Sew tassel at bottom point. Scatter and sew pearls randomly around angel. Slide dowel into casing.

Enlarge 125%

Arms

Make a Joyful Noise

As your guardian angel reminds you to choose joy—
you can help guard the planet with this earth-
friendly tote bag. Make it for your favorite crafter—
it is a perfect size for carrying knitting or crocheting!

What You'll Need

* Tote bag
* Tracing paper and graphite paper
* Pencil
* Cardboard to fit inside tote
* Masking tape
* Acrylic paint: straw, rose chiffon, antique white, flesh, burnt sienna, dusty mauve, black, autumn brown
* Textile medium
* Brushes: 10/0 liner, #6 flat, #10 flat
* Paper towel
* Dimensional fabric paint: sparkles gold, gold glitter

1. Enlarge pattern 133 percent on tracing paper. Insert cardboard into tote bag. Tape sides of design to tote bag, slide graphite paper under design, and trace over lines on pattern, omitting face details and writing.

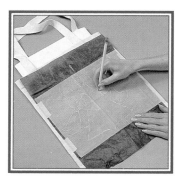

2. Mix all paints with ⅓ textile medium before using, unless other mix is noted. Using #10 brush, basecoat the following: straw on hair, rose chiffon on dress, and antique white on wings. Mix equal parts straw, antique white, and textile medium; paint banner. Mix equal parts rose chiffon, antique white, and textile medium; paint collar. Using #6 brush, basecoat face, neck, and hands with flesh.

3. To shade, dip #6 brush into water and blot softly on paper towel. Dip a corner of brush into paint, blend on a foam plate, apply paint to shaded area. With burnt sienna, shade face, hairline, neck, and where hands meet banner. Using a #10 brush and straw, shade banner at bottom and under hair on right side of banner. Shade dress under and above banner with dusty mauve. Shade collar under hair with rose chiffon.

4. Paint cheeks lightly with dusty mauve, using #6 brush. Let all paint dry. Apply face and verse pattern. Using liner brush and black, paint eyes, nose, mouth, verse, and musical notes. Dipping end of brush into black, make dots on ends of letter lines where indicated.

5. Squeeze sparkles gold paint over dried wing area; spread over wings with #10 brush. Using a mix of autumn brown, straw, and textile medium, add strokes of color to hair with #10 brush. Outline angel with gold glitter paint, dot collar, draw heart, dot bottom of dress, draw lines in hair, and draw halo above head. Let dry 8 hours.

On Angel's Wings

The three-dimensional angel provides an extra touch of elegance to this simple card. The acetate wings lend an ethereal air, and the card's blank interior provides room for a heavenly message.

* 2 pieces white cardstock, 6½ × 9 inches each
* Blue cloud-print paper, 6 × 4¼ inches
* Rubber cement
* Angel stamp (Marks of Distinction)
* Ink pads: black, pink
* Acetate
* Fine-line permanent black marker
* Scissors
* Sponge
* Acrylic paint: light gold, dark gold
* Toothpick
* Heart stamp (Leavenworth Jackson)
* Colored pencils: yellow, pink, peach
* Tape
* Foam mounting tape

1. Fold white cardstock in half to form a card 6½ × 4½ inches. Attach cloud-print paper to front using rubber cement.

2. Stamp angel on second sheet of cardstock, using black ink. Lay acetate over angel and trace around outside of wings with permanent black marker.

3. Cut out wings inside black lines, leaving a longer tab where they will attach to angel's body. Lightly sponge wings with light gold paint. Let dry. With toothpick, use dark gold paint to draw in feathers. Let dry.

4. Stamp heart in pink ink below angel. Cut out heart and angel, cutting off angel's wings.

5. Color angel using colored pencils. Attach acetate wings to back of the angel using tape.

6. Attach angel and heart to front of card using small pieces of foam mounting tape.

Needlepoint Angel Stocking

Add a sparkle to your child's eyes when you give her
this celestial angel stocking for Santa to fill.

* 12 × 20-inch piece blue canvas, #18 mesh
* 1 skein each embroidery floss: brown, yellow, pale peach, rose, pale blue, teal, dark blue, hot pink, white
* Staple gun
* Stretcher bars
* Tapestry needle
* 1 reel gold cable, 10m
* 1 reel each silver and gold ribbon, 1/16 inch wide
* 3 reels each white and lavender ribbon, 1/16 inch wide
* 2 reels yellow medium braid, #16
* Scissors
* Water-erasable marking pen
* Graph paper
* 5/8 yard gold lamé
* 12 × 20-inch piece blue velveteen
* 1½ yard gold lace trim, ¾ inch wide
* 2 yards narrow coral braid trim
* 10 inches gold lace trim, 1½ inches wide

Using staple gun, secure needlepoint canvas to stretcher bars. Locate center of chart and center of canvas. Begin stitching there. Referring to chart, use 1 strand braid, cable, and ribbon to work long stitches, and 6 strands floss to work continental stitches and long stitches where indicated. Use gold cable to work halo and dress. Use yellow braid for all stars. Use yellow floss for hair.

Enlarge stocking pattern on copier by 200 percent; pattern does not include seam allowances. Cut out. Position wrong side of needlepoint stocking on pattern, placing top of pattern 2 inches from tip of upper star. Trace shape onto canvas using marking pen. Cut canvas ½ inch beyond stocking shape. Cut 3 matching stocking shapes from lamé and 1 from velveteen. Baste right side of lamé stocking to wrong side of needlepoint stocking along seam line. With right side of lace on top of right side of stocking, pin and stitch narrow lace trim around stocking. Leave top edge of stocking untrimmed. Sew velveteen backing to needlepoint with right sides together, leaving top edge open for turning. Trim seam allowances to ¼ inch. Clip curves and turn. Press under seam allowance at top.

Pin coral braid around stocking on seam line. Form a hanging loop on right side. Pin wide gold lace across top of stocking; trim to fit. Slipstitch cording and lace in place.

Sew remaining lamé stockings together with right sides facing and leaving top edge open. Sew just inside the ½ inch seam allowance used before. Slip lining inside stocking. Pin under seam allowance at top of lining. Remove lining and press. Reinsert lining and slipstitch in place. Tie a knot in hanging loop, if desired.

Silver
Brown
Gold
White
Pale blue
Dark blue
Pale peach
Yellow
Yellow braid
Rose
Lavender
Teal

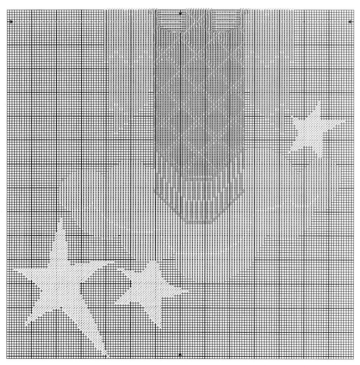

Flying Angel Necklace

Make an easy, fun, and humorous angel to wear
yourself or to give as a gift. If you don't like
necklaces, add a pin back instead and always have
an angel on your shoulder!

What You'll Need

- ✳ 1 piece each Friendly Plastic: purple, red, gold, green, flesh
- ✳ Pencil
- ✳ Scissors
- ✳ Baking sheet (do not use for food)
- ✳ Large sharp needle or tiny drill
- ✳ 12 gold seed beads
- ✳ 28-gauge wire
- ✳ Permanent fine markers for plastic: black, red
- ✳ 2 leaf-shaped jewelry findings, 1⅛ inches each
- ✳ Tacky glue
- ✳ 24 inches red metallic braid, ⅛ inch wide

1. Trace patterns onto plastic and cut out. Use purple for dress, red for halo, gold for wings, green for shoes, and flesh for face and hands. Carefully place on baking sheet so overlapped parts will fuse when heated. On bottom layer have shoes and hands. For next layer place dress. Atop dress place halo and wings. Top layer is face. Layer arm separately, placing hand under arm.

2. Bake for 1½ to 2 minutes in a 250 degree oven. (Hint: Test bake some scraps to check your oven.) Bake until pieces just melt together and edges round a bit. Let cool completely before touching.

3. Use heavy needle or drill to make a hole in arm and body. Thread a seed bead onto center of 2-inch piece of wire. Thread both ends of wire through arm then through body leaving seed bead on top of arm. Twist wire on back and trim. This forms a movable joint.

4. Use black marker to draw eyes, red for mouth. Glue 11 seed beads around head for hair. Let dry. Bend jewelry findings and glue to back of angel to form carrier for necklace. Let dry. Thread braid through carriers and knot ends.

Angelic Vest

Brighten up any outfit with this antique lace and angel charm vest. A little fabric glue and scissors can create quite a fashion statement!

* Linen vest
* Fabric glue
* Straight pins
* 1¼ yards ecru ungathered cluney lace, 1 inch wide
* Hot glue gun and glue sticks
* 1½ yards ivory cording, ½ inch wide
* 5 × 5-inch square antique linen
* 4-inch ecru Irish rose doily
* 8 ivory ribbon roses, 1 inch each
* 12 inches dusty rose French ribbon
* Thin wire
* Scissors
* 1 yard moss sheer ribbon
* Needle and ivory thread
* 5 × 3-inch piece antique lace
* Assorted charms, including angels
* 50 miscellaneous buttons

1. Using fabric glue and straight pins to hold, glue cluney lace around neck and front edge of vest. Use a few drops of hot glue to hold cording into position (see photo for placement), lift up section of cording and glue with fabric glue. Make sure all edges are secured.

2. Using fabric glue, attach linen for pocket and doily to vest. Fabric glue ivory ribbon roses on top of cluney lace. Let dry 24 hours.

3. To make a large ribbon rose, roll French ribbon up in a loose roll and wrap wire around bottom end. To make a 2-loop bow, cut two 5-inch pieces of sheer ribbon. Pinch in center and fold tails in; wrap wire around center. Using a 10-inch piece of sheer ribbon repeat the same process. Sew bows to vest. Sew large ribbon rose to large sheer bow. Glue to vest with fabric glue.

4. Pinch bottom of antique lace and sew to vest. Sew angel charm over bottom of lace. Using hot glue put a drop of glue on buttons and position them. Put a drop of hot glue on charms and position them. Hand sew all buttons and charms to vest. Reinforce any loose areas with fabric glue. Let dry.

Pretty Patty Treetopper

Top your tree with this pretty angel—her homemade charm and lacy elegance will make her a family favorite. This could be a lovely gift for newlyweds to start their collection of Christmas decorations!

49

* 2 doilies, 8 inches each
* Scissors
* Waxed paper
* White craft glue
* Toothpicks
* 6-inch styrofoam cone
* 1½-inch porcelain doll parts
* Paring knife
* Straight pins
* 1 can spray stiffener
* 2 rubber bands
* Hot glue gun and glue sticks
* 15 inches gold ribbon, ¼ inch wide
* Wire cutters
* 4 gold ribbon roses, ½ inch each

1. Clip a 1-inch-diameter hole in center of a doily. Lay doily on waxed paper and apply white craft glue to edges of cut out center.

2. Stick 2 or 3 toothpicks in top of foam cone. Place porcelain head over toothpicks. If head wobbles,

use paring knife to thin top of cone.

3. Slip center hole of doily over angel's head. Press glued edge of doily to top of doll's torso.

4. Arrange deep folds in doily. Pin bottom of folds to cone to keep folds in place. Place on waxed paper and spray with stiffener. Rearrange folds as needed. Let dry.

5. Cut another piece (about 11 inches long) of waxed paper. Place rubber bands on each end of the remaining roll.

6. Lay out last doily on waxed paper piece. Spray with stiffener until soaked. Place waxed paper roll across center of doily, folding half of doily over roll. Let dry.

7. To form wings, fold top half of doily back up to center fold so the edge extends a little beyond the center fold. Hot glue in place. Hot glue wings behind head.

8. Remove pins and take angel from styrofoam cone. Find holes in dress to push arms through. Make sure placement looks reasonable before you glue in place. Turn over and apply hot glue to underside of angel dress, where arms stick through, to hold arms.

9. Make ¾- to 1-inch bow from ¼-inch gold ribbon. Hot glue under chin. Trim ends of ribbon.

10. Use wire cutters to cut off wire close to bottom of roses. Hot glue roses to folds of dress at bottom.

Starry Angel Shelf

Add to your heavenly decor with this angel shelf. Its stencil stars and lace angel will brighten any room!

Listening Hearts Hear Angels Sing!

What You'll Need

* Wood shelf (unassembled)
* White pickling
* Brush
* Star and moon stencil
* Drafting tape
* Stencil paint: metallic silver, wedgewood blue
* 2 stencil brushes
* Paper towels
* 2 plastic bags
* 15 × 19-inch white linen battenburg lace tea towel
* Waxed paper
* 2¼-inch wood ball knob
* Acrylic paint: medium flesh, black
* Stylus
* 5-inch square white battenburg lace doily
* Scissors
* Tacky glue
* Fine point tweezers
* 60 inches blue satin ribbon, 1/16 inch wide
* 1½-inch white satin bow
* 71 inches silver star garland
* Low-temp glue gun and glue sticks
* 5/8-inch eye screw
* 10 inches white satin ribbon, 1/16 inch wide
* 7-inch wood heart
* Wood varnish
* Permanent black marker
* 23 inches gathered lace, 1 inch wide
* 6 white ribbon roses on ribbon

1. Test pickling on back of wood piece. Adjust color if needed. There is no need to seal wood when finished. Work quickly and avoid brush strokes over drying paint. Paint all pieces of shelf (top shelf, side piece, pegs, and plugs) with white pickling. Allow to dry.

2. Tape stencil to top of shelf. Place moon at center of shelf top. Dip dry stencil brush into silver stencil paint. Blot brush on paper towel until excess paint is removed. There should only be a hint of paint left on brush. Using a circular motion and starting at edges, stencil in moon. Place brush in plastic bag to keep brush from drying out. Dip second dry stencil brush into blue stencil paint. Repeat process of removing excess paint from brush. Stencil stars. Allow a minute for paint to dry and remove stencil from shelf top.

3. Stencil stars with blue paint on front of shelf. Allow a minute for paint to dry and remove stencil.

4. Flip shelf top. Stencil stars with blue paint on bottom of shelf top. Allow a minute for paint to dry and remove

stencil. Place brush in plastic bag. Clean stencil with soap and water. Assemble shelf.

5. Wash and iron tea towel. Place tea towel right side up on waxed paper. Tape tea towel to work surface. Tape stencil to tea towel, placing moon to left side of tea towel. Stencil in moon with silver paint. Fill in the rest of tea towel bottom with blue stars. Let dry. Remove stencil. Remove tea towel.

6. Paint wood knob with flesh. Allow to dry. Dot black eyes with stylus. Let dry.

7. To make angel arms, take one top corner of tea towel and make a knot. Pull knot secure. Repeat process for other top corner. There will be a 5- to 6-inch gap between knots.

8. Cut a small X in center of 5-inch doily. Find center of tea towel between knots and pull into a 1-inch point. Pull point through cut on doily. Angel will begin to take shape. Apply a small amount of glue to hole at bottom of head. Using tweezers, insert point of tea towel into hole. Let glue set.

9. Cut blue ribbon into 2 equal pieces. Tie ribbon around neckline and secure with knot. Glue white bow over knot in ribbon. Trim ribbon.

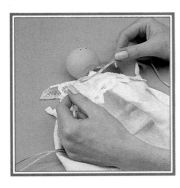

10. From silver star garland, form a 2¼-inch-diameter circle at one end. Loop remaining garland around circle to form halo. With remaining garland, make wings. Bend garland into a tear-shaped 10-inch loop, securing loop with a few twists. Continue garland to opposite side and make a second 10-inch tear-shaped loop and secure with a twist. Repeat 2 more loops (1 on each side) and secure end of garland to center of wings. Glue halo and wings to angel with low-temp glue.

11. Screw eye screw into center top of head. Cut white ribbon into 6-inch and 4-inch pieces. Thread 6-inch piece of white ribbon through eye screw and knot off.

12. Rub blue stencil paint onto wood heart with brush. Wipe excess paint off with paper towel. Seal heart with varnish. Let dry. Write saying on heart with black marker and knob-and-pole printing (see page 11). Glue lace to back of heart. Glue roses onto heart. Make a small hole at center top of heart. Apply glue into hole and insert 4-inch piece of ribbon. Let dry.

Angelic Clay Ornaments

These dangling angel ornaments are fun to make
and even more fun to hang on the tree. Make
an angel for each member of your family—change
hair color and lengths to personalize!

* Polymer clay: fleshtone, red, white, green, black
* Toothpicks
* Pointed knife
* Wire paper clips
* Wire cutters
* Ruler
* Garlic press
* Baking sheet
* White craft glue, craft brush
* 5/0 red sable brush
* Toffee acrylic paint
* Waterbase gloss varnish for polymer clay
* ½-inch brush
* 8 inches green or red ribbon, ⅛ inch wide

1. Work the clay in your hand to soften it, then roll it into a coil. From fleshtone, make a 1-inch-high egg shape (with flat back) for head. Use tip of toothpick to sculpt eyes, nose, and mouth. Add small balls and snakes (thinly rolled coil of clay) to build up forehead, nose, cheeks, and eyes. Refine the face. Make small snakes of red clay for lips.

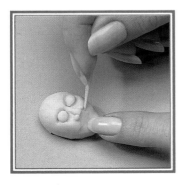

2. Snip off loop of paper clip. Push open ends of larger loop into top of head.

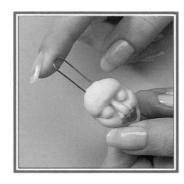

3. From white clay, roll about 14 snakes, each with a point on one end. Cut them in varying lengths, from 1¼ to 2½ inches long. The longer snakes will be at the top of the wings. Blending the blunt end of each snake into the angel head, arrange snakes into wings. Gently press each snake into the one above it.

4. Use garlic press to make hair in color of your choice. Arrange hair on angel head.

5. Using green, make 6 or 7 holly leaves. Arrange them in a semicircle. Gently press them into each other.

6. Break a toothpick in half. Balance the halves on top of the paper clip, next to the head. They act as a support for the holly leaf halo as the piece bakes.

7. Slide knife under holly leaf halo and place on angel's head. Gently press holly leaf tips next to face into hair.

8. Make several tiny red holly berries. Place 3 on each leaf tip next to face and 1 at top center. Gently press balls onto leaves.

9. Bake at 200 degrees for 2 hours. A long baking time with a low temperature is recommended so that the white wings won't scorch and the thick head is still baked all the way through. Let cool. (Be sure to keep all utensils used with clay for nonfood purposes only!)

10. Turn over and rub white glue into the area where wings and hair meet. Let dry.

11. Using 5/0 brush, paint on eyelashes with toffee paint. Let dry. Using ½-inch brush, coat with varnish. Let dry 24 hours.

12. Thread 8 inches of ribbon through paper clip. Tie an overhand knot near the open end for a hanger.

God Bless Angel Doll

Everyone needs a doll and a guardian angel—
combine both with this loving and lovely angel doll.
She isn't to be played with, but she will be
treasured forever!

* 15-inch doll with blond hair attached, undressed
* 2 tea bags
* ½ yard muslin
* 2 ecru pineapple design doilies, 10 inches round
* Liquid fabric stiffener
* Dimensional fabric paint: sparkles gold
* 1-inch sponge brush
* Gold and crystal glitter with stars
* Blush (powder make-up with brush)
* Iron
* Scissors
* Sewing machine
* Piece of cardboard
* Black fine-point permanent marker
* 24 inches ecru satin ribbon
* Green Spanish moss
* Hot glue gun, glue sticks
* 6 dried-look small pink silk roses with leaves
* 12-inch small white bell silk flowers
* Small bundle pink pepperberries
* 6-inch string ecru pearls
* 25 to 30 old buttons various shapes, colors, and sizes
* Needle with ecru thread

1. Heat water in pot with 2 tea bags; let sit 2 minutes. Dip muslin into tea and soak for 2 minutes; remove muslin and line dry or place in dryer. Heavily coat 1 doily with liquid fabric stiffener. Let air dry flat, about 3 hours. When stiff, paint one side of doily with sparkles gold fabric paint. Apply heavily, using sponge brush. Sprinkle crystal star glitter on wet doily. Let dry 1 to 2 hours. Shake off excess glitter.

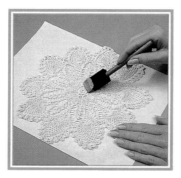

2. Dust doll cheeks with blush make-up. Press muslin with hot iron. Tear two 1-inch-wide strips, the length of the material. Cut one strip in half and tie half strips into 2½-inch-wide bows for sleeves. Tie other strip into a 4-inch-wide bow for back of wings. Enlarge dress pattern 200 percent. Fold muslin in half, then in half again. Place shoulders and front of dress on folds, and trace lightly. Cut out dress. Fray bottom edge of dress.

3. Turn dress inside out. Using machine or by hand, sew both sides of dress and up under arms. Turn right side out. Lay dress flat, and insert cardboard inside of dress. Using permanent marker, write verse on bottom of dress. Measuring from raw edge of neck down ⅛ inch, sew a running stitch around neck, leaving strings on both ends to tie. Put dress on doll. Tighten string around neck and knot. Repeat procedure for sleeves.

4. Pull hair up on top of head making a ponytail and tie with 7-inch strip of satin ribbon. Trim tails. Wrap moss to form a 4-inch strip and hot glue onto top of head around ponytail. Glue leaves, roses, white flowers, and pepperberries into moss.

5. Cut unstiffened doily in half, turn cut edge under and hot glue around doll's neck. Hot glue pearls around neck. Hot glue buttons on doily creating a cascading effect by overlapping some buttons.

6. Turn doll over. Using a generous amount of hot glue, glue center of stiff doily at the center top of shoulders, placing glittered side of doily against back. Fold 15-inch piece ribbon in half, creating a loop. Hot glue ends of ribbon to center of doily. When glue is dry, hot glue 4-inch muslin bow across ribbon ends. Hot glue a ¾-inch-round button across ribbon, about 2 inches above bow. Hot glue 2½-inch bows at each sleeve.

7. Using needle and thread, sew hands together. Hot glue pepperberries over hands in cascading design. Hot glue roses, white bell flowers, and leaves into pepperberries. Hot glue a button on each shoe.

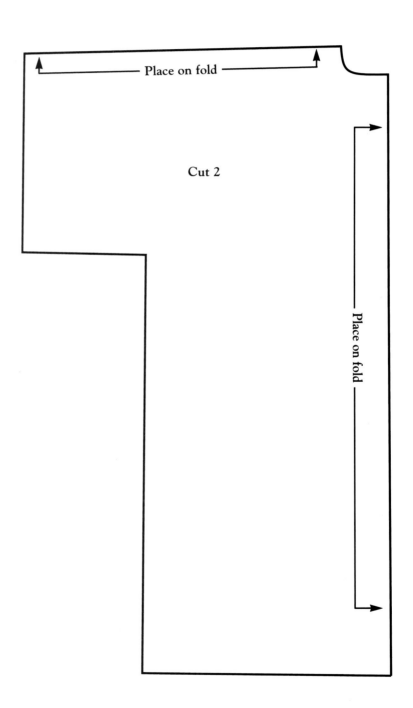

Place on fold

Cut 2

Place on fold

Dancing Among the Stars

Stars cascade over the tops of these angel
ornaments—a welcome addition to any
Christmas tree.

What You'll Need

* ✻ 11 × 14-inch sheet clear plastic canvas, #10 mesh
* ✻ 1 skein each embroidery floss: brown, rust, black, pale peach
* ✻ 2 skeins each embroidery floss: yellow, teal, purple, tangerine
* ✻ 3 skeins each embroidery floss: white
* ✻ Embroidery floss scraps: green, brown, blue, rose
* ✻ 1 reel gold cable, 10m
* ✻ Scissors
* ✻ Tapestry needle
* ✻ 1 yard gold wire, 28-gauge
* ✻ 1 package gold rochaille beads
* ✻ 2 packages amethyst stars, 11mm
* ✻ 1 package gold stars, 22mm

Use 10-strand lengths to stitch designs with continental stitch. Use 4 strands gold cable to stitch halos. For eyes and mouths, use 10 strands to work French knots, wrapping floss around needle once. Dots on face indicate where to insert and reinsert needle.

For braids, thread needle with 12 strands brown floss. Insert needle at lower left of X, leaving 3½ inches of floss; bring needle up at upper right on X. Trim floss even with 3½-inch length. Repeat procedure for remaining part of X. There will be a total of 48 strands of floss. Split strands into 3 bundles of 16 and braid for 1½ inches. Wrap end with a short strand of matching floss. Use 8 strands white to overcast edges.

For star garlands, cut wire into three 12-inch lengths. Thread needle with wire and insert through threads on back of angel; twist to secure. Pull needle up through dot on hand; wrap around bar.

Thread wire with 20 rochaille beads, 1 amethyst star, 15 rochaille beads, 1 gold star, 15 rochaille beads, 1 amethyst star, and 20 rochaille beads. Insert wire on opposite hand, wrap around bar, and secure on back.

■	Brown
■	Rust
■	Black
□	Yellow
■	Peach
■	Teal
■	Tangerine
■	Purple
■	Red
□	White
■	Gold
■	Green
■	Blue

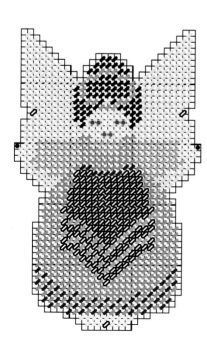
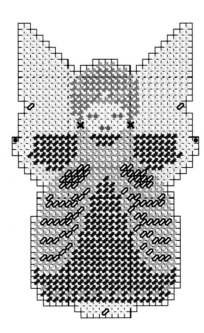
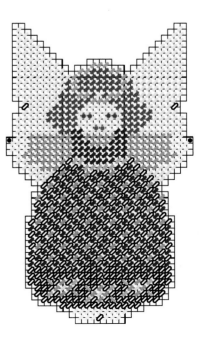

A Ring of Angels

Ring your Christmas tree with angels! It's hard to believe that this exquisite and opulent tree skirt is a breeze to make. The rich gold cording and gold lamé will make this a cherished family possession!

* 54-inch round felt hunter green tablecloth
* Scissors
* Iron
* 2 yards fabric adhesive
* 3 squares antique white felt
* 2 squares flesh felt
* 3 squares red felt
* ½ yard gold lamé
* Pencil
* Dimensional fabric paint: sparkles gold, gold glitter, ivory pearl, green glitter
* Brushes: #8 flat, 10/0 liner
* Fabric glue
* 5 yards small gold rickrack
* Acrylic paint: rose, black
* 2 yards thin gold cord
* 8 yards fancy gold trim, ¾ inch wide

1. Cut a straight line to center of tablecloth. Cut out a 4-inch circle for tree.

2. Iron adhesive to back of felt squares and lamé, using medium setting. Press for 4 to 5 seconds. Trace patterns on paper. There are 5 angels on tree skirt, 5 stars to hold, and 30 scattered stars. Use antique white for face, hands, and feet; flesh for hair; red for dress; and gold lamé for stars. Cut out and remove paper.

3. Position first angel on skirt. Iron appliqués to felt. Evenly space remaining angels around skirt and adhere. Iron on both shapes of stars. Spread sparkles gold paint over wings with flat brush.

4. Outline hair, stars, and wings with gold glitter paint. Draw on shoes and halo with gold glitter paint. Outline face and hands with ivory pearl.

5. Glue gold rickrack around dresses and sleeves, using fabric glue. Glue a strip of rickrack across dresses.

6. Lightly paint cheeks on face with rose paint using flat brush. Using liner brush and black, paint eyes. Using green glitter paint, draw holly on dress. Using ivory pearl, dot dress around holly and dot buttons on sleeve. Divide gold cord into 10 pieces. Tie 2 small bows for each angel from gold cord and glue to waist and at tail of dress. Using fabric glue, attach fancy trim around tree skirt and around center hole. Let dry 4 hours.

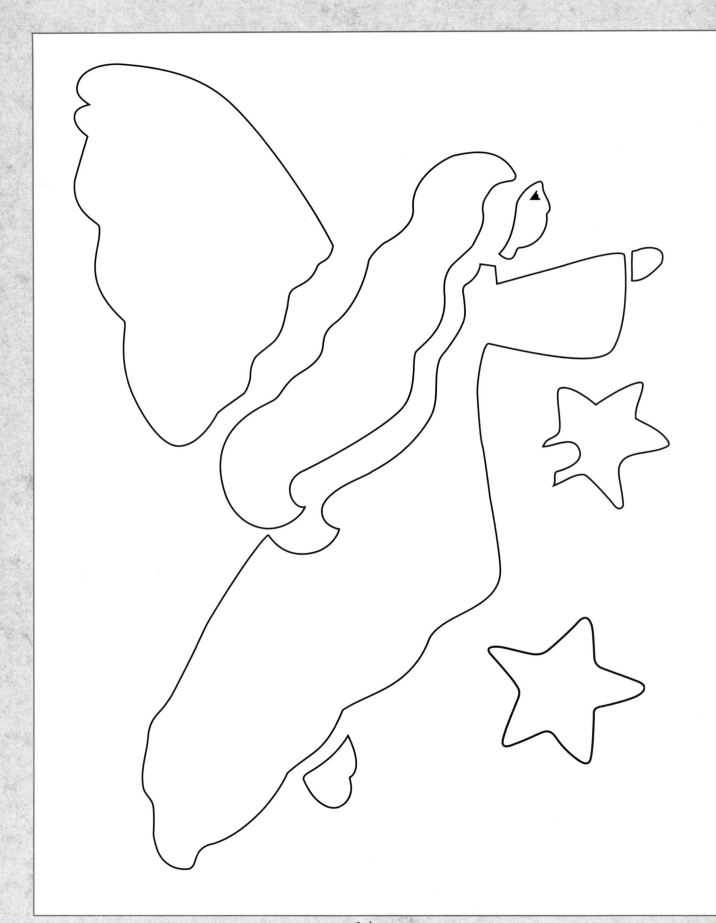